A LIGHT GREEN LIGHT
TOWARD SUSTAINABILITY IN PRACTICE

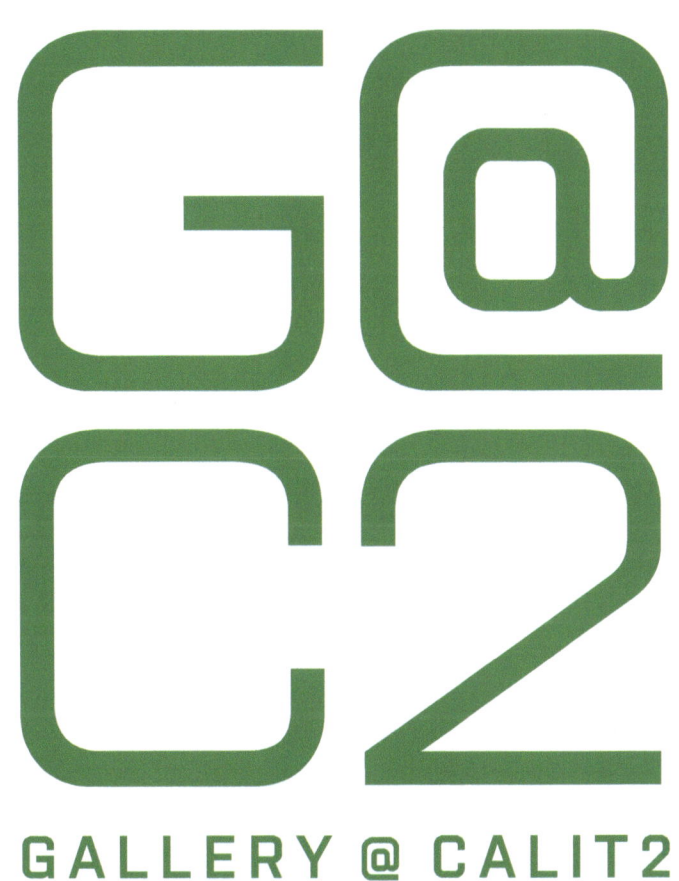

GALLERY @ CALIT2

GALLERY@CALIT2
EXHIBITION CATALOG N°9

A LIGHT GREEN LIGHT
TOWARD SUSTAINABILITY IN PRACTICE
INSTALLATIONS BY SABRINA RAAF

GALLERY INSTALLATION
APRIL 20, 2010 TO JUNE 4, 2010

Copyright 2010 by the gallery@calit2

Published by the gallery@calit2

University of California, San Diego
9500 Gilman Drive
La Jolla, CA 92093-0436

ISBN 978-0-578-06223-5

CONTENTS

INTRODUCTION

BY JORDAN CRANDALL

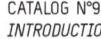

Sabrina Raaf's exhibition in the gallery@ calit2, A Light Green Light: Toward Sustainability in Practice, comes at a time when it could be said that we're witnessing an important turn in art and theory: a turn toward "ecological" models of production and interpretation. This ecological turn occurs in conjunction with another important strand of contemporary thought: "object-oriented" philosophical pursuits.

Like all turns in art and theory, this one is accompanied by very real societal changes. We glimpse these changes in the emergence of terms like "sustainability." Sustainability indicates new forms of being in the world where humans are no longer separate from the environments that uphold them. It references the need for new ways of thinking about our interdependency with nature – ways of apprehending the world that no longer rely on human/nature, or subject/object divides, and which instead seek to articulate forms of agency that span these categorical distinctions.

This ecological turn is not about a return. It's not about a return to a romantic idea of a past unsullied by technological change. Rather, it is a call for concepts that work in conjunction with technological change – concepts that can allow us to work across the biological, the technological, and the urban, capturing the dynamic interrelation of processes and objects, beings and things, patterns and matter.

Through such ways of thinking, we can explore how elements of complex systems, whether human, technological, natural, can "cooperate" across many different domains of contemporary life to produce new assemblages – hybrid entities that can bring together, and redistribute, the faculties of humans, machines, and things. We're not only talking about forms of thinking, but also forms of existence, forms of being, forms of living.

In all of these regards Sabrina Raaf has an exemplary practice.

We are at a time in history when the interpretation itself has to be as inventive as the work, its analysis as novel as its material form. And so in considering this work I hope we will take the time to experiment, to improvise, to respond to the CO2 levels in the room just like Raaf's Translator II: Grower, an assemblage that does not simply respond to a level but to a rhythm, the collective rhythms of the drawing in and out of the breath, that most vital corporeal function, which complicates the boundaries between body and environment, melding as it does biological needs and cultural effects.

Breathe.

ESSAY
TOWARD SUSTAINABILITY IN PRACTICE
BY STEVE DIETZ

I first experienced one of Sabrina Raaf's works, Saturday, at the 2004 ISEA in Tallinn, Estonia. To listen to Saturday, which is a mix of surveilled conversations from a neighborhood park, you don't put on headphones, you put on a glove. The glove has a bone transducer in it, which transmits the audio by touching your forehead.

I remember being amazed at the time, when I realized I was listening through my fingers. It was magic. Prestidigitation. But as I listened to the conversations – snatches of drug deals and amorous entreaties and errands to run before coming home – the interface became increasingly sensical, almost inevitable. It was a sleight of hand that distracted me from the fact of the theft of the conversations. It made physical the virtual communications in the ether surrounding us, which, even if they are apparently invisible, are subject to being caught. And whether they would end up in benign hands could not be guaranteed. But what the interface never became, despite its sophistication, was about the technology.

I experienced this same blend of nerdy, magical, glamorous, righteous pragmatism when I first met Sabrina in the summer of 2009. In a quiet voice that was conspiratorial only in the sense that it assumed I understood what she was talking about, she explained her plans for what was to become Meandering River, and Hans-Henrik Stølum's 1996 article "River Meandering as a Self-Organization Process." Of course, I knew it, I nodded. Photographs and diagrams of Poulsen lamps transmogrified into mosquito netting via origami sites and a particular NASA video she had recently found. "Inspirations" for the work ranged from high tech jewelry to an illuminated umbrella powered by rain to a virtual tensegrity site by SodaPlay. Her dew harvesting proposal for (n)-fold was based, in part, on the experience of the International Organization for Dew Utilization as well as Ned Kahn's Articulated Cloud for the Pittsburgh Children's Museum.

In other words, Sabrina's sources ranged far and wide from academic journals on the environment and robotics to real-world solutions – or at least experiments - by the hobbyist and the well-funded lab alike to the inter-penetrating worlds of art, architecture, design, craft, and engineering. Her joy in her topic(s) of choice as well as the rigor with which she approached them was contagious.

Sustainable Practice

There are many different ways to understand "sustainability in practice," but perhaps the baseline requirement is "sustained inquiry." It is not redundant to say that in order for a practice to be sustainable, it must be sustained. Sustainability is not just an end point, it is a daily, ongoing long-term practice, in "sickness and in health," that "neither snow nor rain nor heat nor gloom of night" can stay, so to speak. I suppose this can be viewed as a hopelessly naïve and romantic view of the artist, more akin to starving in one's garret than being an actor in a network or an economic agent or a researcher among researchers, but I think the evidence of Sabrina's practice over many decades, which is by no means unique, is that it is

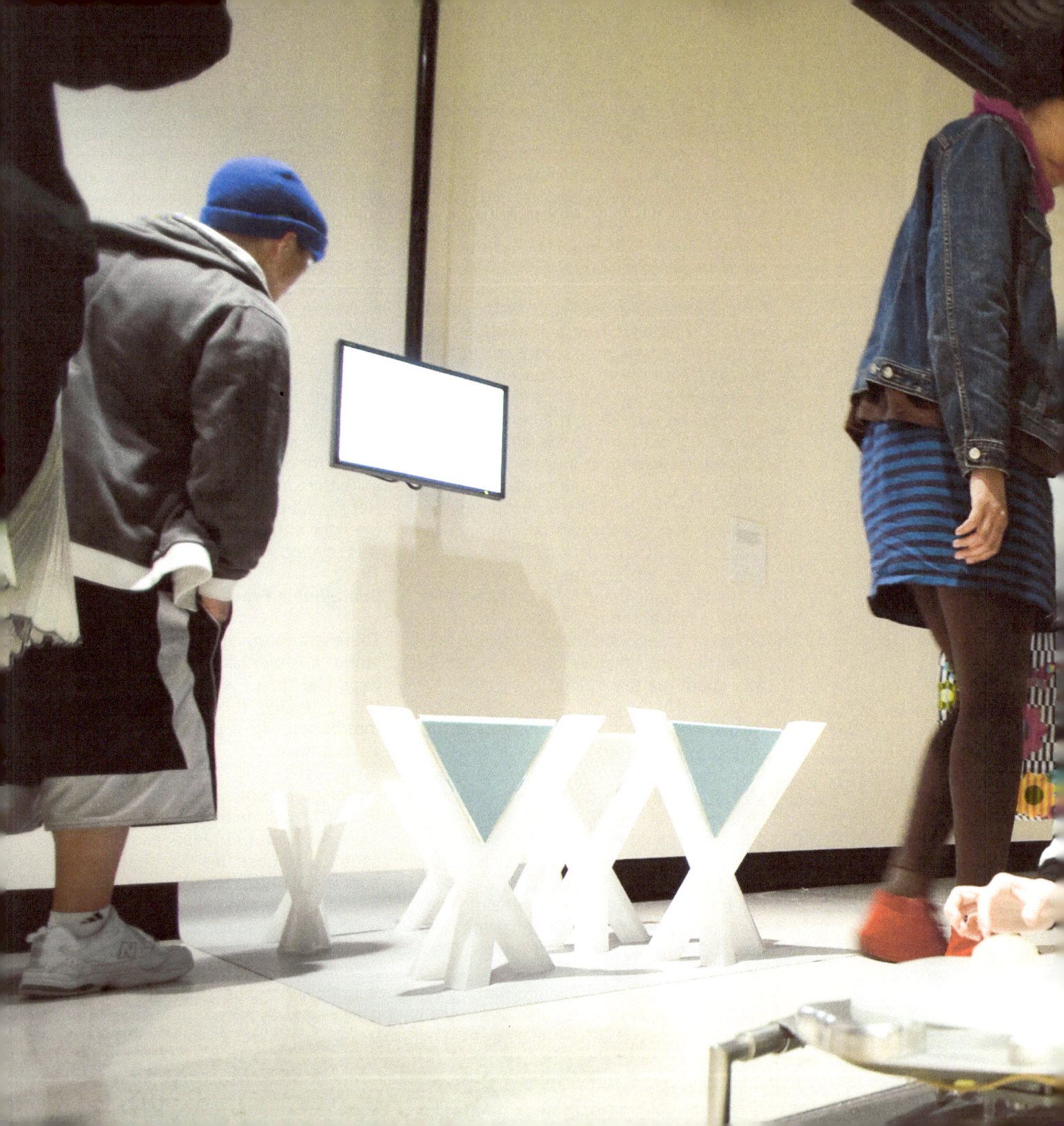

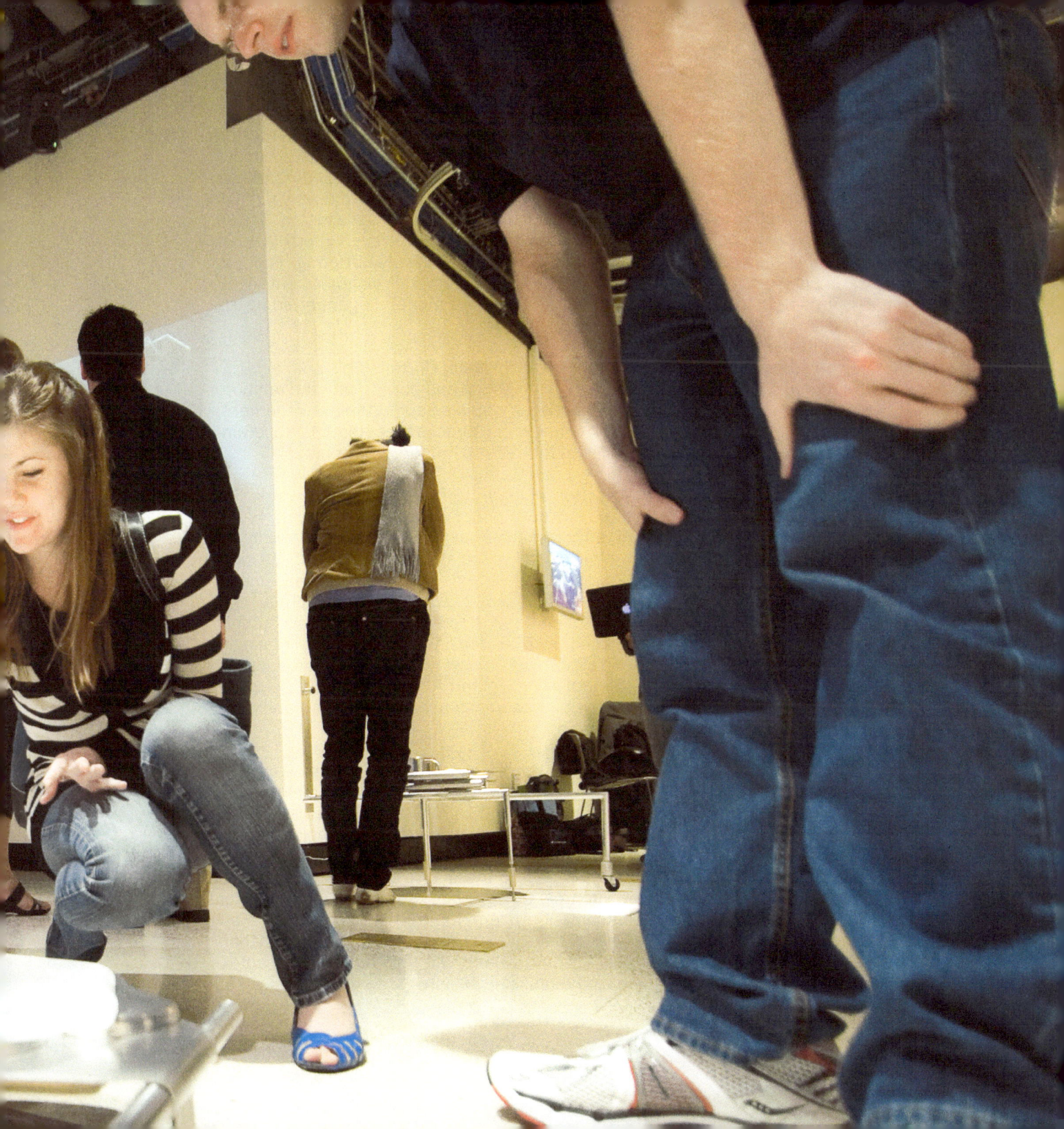

sustained. The issue of how to continue to make it so is not just economic or even existential, it is ecological.

The "science of relationships between organisms and their environment" is how Sabrina quotes Ernst Haeckel as defining ecology, and when I say that the issue of a sustainable practice is ecological, I don't just mean that it is about the environment, as noble and as important as such a cause might be. Sabrina's practice, like any artist's, can only be sustained – and understood – as relational to an unruly set of fields of knowledge and practical expertise. It cannot and should not be defined solely in the context of art or "new media," whatever that is, or art and technology or computation or environmental studies or agriculture or CNC systems or space or river morphology or robotics or public health or origami. Sabrina's practice is a sustained inquiry into and between and among.

Light Green Light, of course, does encompass a particular set of five artworks, which have differing but not unrelated relationships to a particular set of ideas, which can be understood, perhaps, as sustainability in the environmental sense.

Practicing Sustainability

Sabrina continues to make work that does not directly address environmental sustainability issues, such as her recent Curtain Wall (2009), in which a hanging sculptural environment "recreates the facade of the McCormick Place West building and bends its structure until it takes on the form of a pliable curtain, blowing in the wind." As with Translator II: Grower, which is in the Light Green Light exhibition, Curtain Wall is an environmental work in that it is a responsive environment. As Sabrina writes about it: "In keeping with the original meaning of the Windy City moniker (based upon blustery politics and politicians), the virtual 'glass curtain' shown in the video reacts to voice levels (both in their pitch and volume) by actively fluttering, floating, or flapping. The more 'wind' visitors create with their voices the more motion is generated in the curtain."

In the broadest sense, Curtain Wall is an ecological work highlighting and playing with the relationships between organisms and their environment, but it is not in any direct sense about the sustainability of the natural-human environment.

With her Icelandic Rift (2006-2007) series, Sabrina did/does directly/indirectly deal with issues of environmental sustainability by encouraging the viewer to speculate with her about not only how agriculture – and mineral extraction? – might happen in a zero gravity environment but why. Overpopulation? Nuclear holocaust? Economic enrichment? Divorce? As with much challenging – and sustaining – artwork, the motivation is left up to the viewer. Iceland Rift is a platform as much for the human imagination as agricultural experimentation.

What is distinguishing – and challenging - about the new series of works that includes Meandering River, n-(fold), and Light Green Light is that while they retain a speculative aspect like Icelandic Rift, the speculation is more pragmatically experimental. How best to thermally insulate a constructed environment. How best to create a rainwater catchment system for arid environments. How best to design "a lamp that could do more than just light, but that could also unpack into a flexible, minimalist living environment."

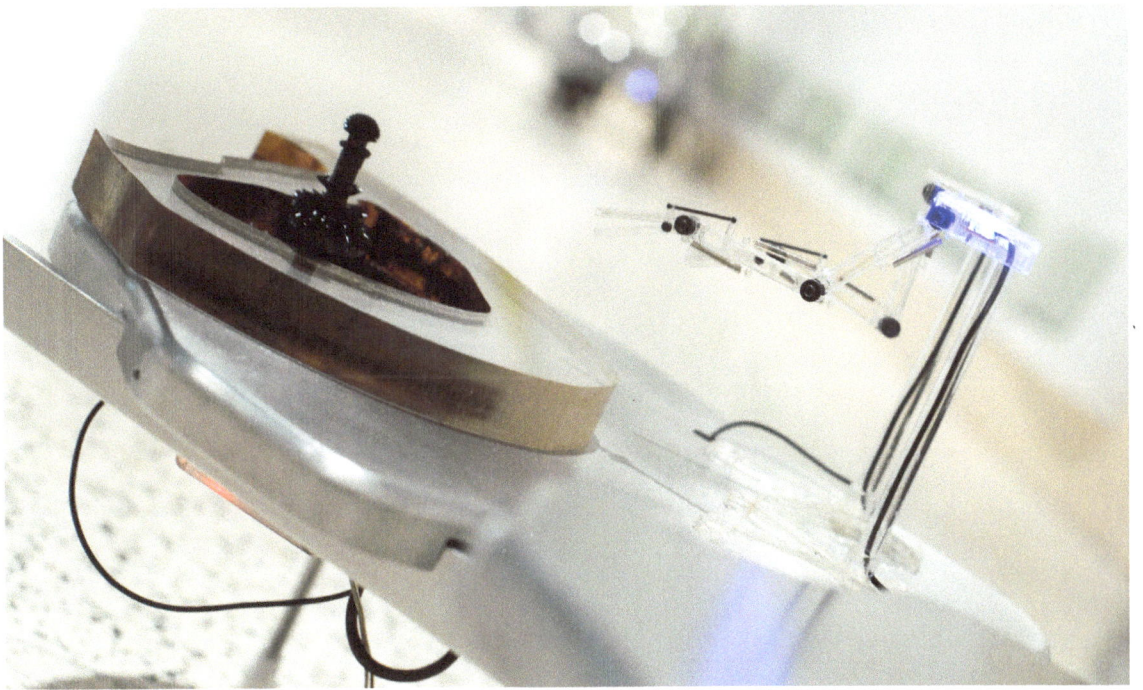

It is the criteria for "best" that interests me. Along with saving the world, of course. Why a meandering river pattern for the transpiration of the thermal screens? Why high-end Danish designs for the look of the dew harvester and lamp-net? The easy answer, I suppose, is that they look good. A beautiful marriage of design and functionality. But I'm not buying it. Isn't there something more?

Probing Practice

The artist duo Dunne + Raby, in their practice and teaching, emphasize critical design as a form of research, not to make "better" products but as often as not to explore contemporary society by designing imagine-able products, "launching them," and studying the results (see Dunne + Raby, Design Noir: The Secret Life of Electronic Objects). It is this probing of the ecology of organisms' our relationship to their environment that Sabrina's work shares with Dunne + Raby and many others. Light Green Light, the exhibition, is about the human-natural environment, yes. It is about sustainability in a world of excess and need, yes. But at its core, it is about sustaininig a practice that sends out beautiful probes to provoke a reaction by us to our environments - large and small, universal and personal – which in turn affects the environment of the artist, who is already practicing her next probe.

Practice. Practice. Practice.

ESSAY
LIGHT GREEN LIGHT
BY SABRINA RAAF

The sculptural forms created for the Light Green Light series were inspired by mobile, sustainable, and modular architectural systems. I've long been fascinated by spaces such as Buckminster Fuller's Dymaxion House which can be mechanically shifted and/or transmuted on-the-fly in order to accommodate varying functions and inhabitants. These designs inspired me to begin my practice ten years ago in creating interactive, machine-based installations capable of sensing the space around them, reacting to it, and rendering a record of the life within.

To this point, I've designed sculptures to respond to levels of automated activity in a building, the light as it shifts in a room, the amount of carbon dioxide that visitors exhale, and the pitch and amplitude of inhabitants' voices. The audio-visual record(s) generated by my sculptures have thereby both reflected and amplified evidence of the changing states of a space. Such changes have also included shifts in usage of a space and whether such shifts occurred as rapid or gradual, as unpredictable or regular, as transitory, or as evolutionary in nature. My interest continues to lie in the defining of new ways in which art, in the form of responsive environments, might inform a community about the social space they share and of the uniqueness of their presence and their moment within it.

My research shifted focus with the start of the Light Green Light series towards integrating sustainable design methodologies into more environmentally conscientious (though still functional) art works. I was motivated by the level to which sustainable practices have increased cross-disciplinary dialog among scientists, artists, and designers. The mixing of art and ecology has accelerated a growth of new visual topologies wherein aesthetics become naturally folded into 'green' sensibilities and environmental activism is crossbred with responsive design. I've found artists and designers have become increasingly focused on how their objects can mesh into greater natural ecologies. Their objects often have what I would call 'metabolic properties' in that they are capable of flourishing, maturing, and decaying alongside the environment they are placed in. It's been fascinating to watch how these ideas are pushing boundaries within our culture - critically redefining them by forcing both an expansion of aesthetic terrain and the rise of new art and design centers which have embraced the course of ecological awareness and a perishable sensibility.

There are several questions I considered while conceiving of the Light Green Light series. The first is whether or not artworks designed to modify their behavior in response to fluctuating environmental conditions could motivate a spectator to similarly act to modify their behavior in response to fluctuations in the environment. Next, to what degree could art impart a deeper awareness of the environment as 'shared space' along with imparting the tools that would enable the viewer to build their own approach to sustainable practices? Last, could the gallery environment be – despite its iconically unnatural, white-walled and even austere characteristics – an appropriate and viable space in which to address issues of the natural environment today?

Translator II: Grower, 2004-6

Dimensions: 2'h x 2'w x 17"d
Materials: custom mechanics, aluminum, sensors, and ink

Funding: This project was made possible by a grant from the Creative Capital foundation in NYC

As to the consideration of the gallery as a site for addressing ecological matters, this was a question on which I first addressed with the piece, Translator II: Grower. Ernst Haeckel (1834 –1919), the 19th century German philosopher, biologist, and artist, famously defined ecology as the "science of relationships between organisms and their environment." With this in mind, I considered how to apply the basic principles of his ecological model layout to a gallery system. As institutions, galleries (along with museums) serve on a social level as forums for cultural display, pedagogy, and for critical dialog between artists and audiences interested in both aesthetics and social-political issues. Through Haeckel's model, one could envision the gallery as host environment to an active array of organisms (artists, curators, art audiences, collectors, and artwork) which have over time, developed a complex set of symbiotic relationships with one another as well as to the gallery. My goal with Translator II: Grower was to make the relationship between the gallery habitat and its inhabitants visible, and to look for a means to express their social patterns and the feedback-based relations that exist within the gallery's ecological niche.

The sculpture Translator II: Grower is the resulting mechanism of this investigation.

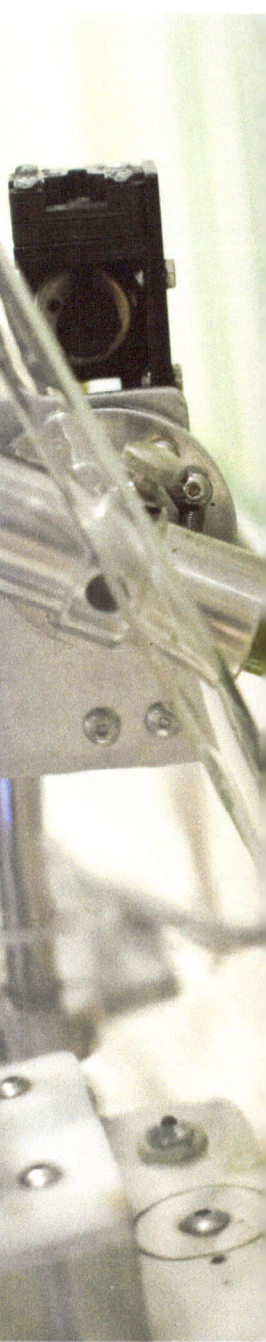

Grower is a small 'rover' vehicle that navigates along a gallery's walls and responds to the carbon dioxide level in the air by drawing blades of 'grass' on the walls in green ink. The Grower robot senses the carbon dioxide (CO_2) level in the air via a small digital sensor mounted high on a wall of the exhibition space. Every few seconds, it takes a reading of the CO_2 level and then draws a blade of grass on the wall. The number of inhabitants and visitors in the exhibit space breathing in oxygen and exhaling CO_2 has an immediate effect on the drawings. The blade height pertains directly to the level of CO_2 (and therefore also the level of attendance) in the space. The more CO_2, the higher the grass is drawn (with a maximum height of one foot) Once Grower completes a line, it moves forward several millimeters and repeats the process. By the end of an exhibition, the lower portion of a gallery's wall is covered with fine green lines which together resemble a cross-section of a field of grass.

In nature, grass needs CO_2 to grow and us humans participate in this overall system by adding to the available CO_2 level through lung filtration of oxygen from CO_2 by breathing. Grower also needs humans – specifically gallery inhabitants and visitors - in order to grow (through drawing) its fields of grass. The health of the grass fields is a direct reflection of the level of human presence and participation within the gallery space. The feedback-based relationship expressed by the Grower therefore is that the more warm life present in the gallery, the greater the likelihood of that gallery to flourish and to foster the creation of new life – i.e., new communi-

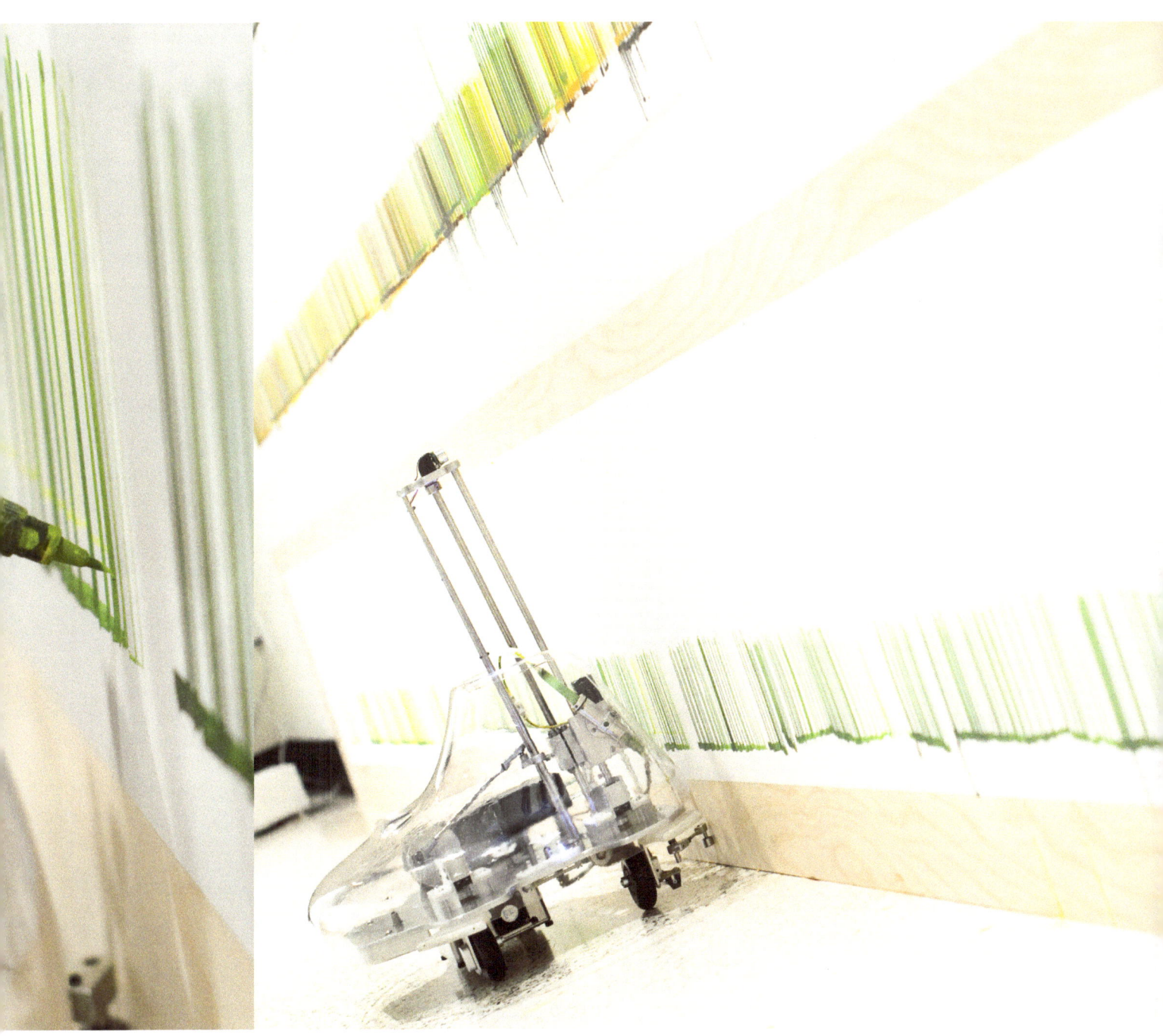

ties and new artwork. Poetically speaking then, the suggestion is that the relationship between the gallery habitat and its inhabitants is a cross-metabolic one in nature. The Grower merely makes visible the degree to which art institutions depend on the presence of their staff and of visitors to make them healthy spaces within which new ecologies of art may evolve and flourish.

Meandering River, 2009-10
Materials: Robotically-etched, thermal screen made from recyclable HDPE, with vinyl application
Dimensions: 24" wide x length variable

In the fall of 2009, I had the honor of becoming the first artist-in-residence at Gibotech Scandinavia A/S, an international company specializing in the development of robotics applications. The residency provided me with the opportunity to incorporate Gibotech's robotic expertise and hardware into the production of a site-specific artwork. Because I had virtually no familiarity with their robotic technology in advance of the residency, I began the project planning by delineating a greater conceptual/ organizational framework for the development of a new piece. This included the defining of three main design principles on which to focus: structural versatility, open source design, and variability of function.

As to the aesthetic/artistic content of the work, Denmark's unique geography provided the primary source of inspiration. Denmark is a nation comprised of a large peninsula, five major islands, and literally hundreds of minor islands. It is a nation therefore surrounded by sea and traversed by a vast network of canals, rivers, lakes, and watersheds. Over millennia, these waterways have etched complex patterns into the Danish landscape. Intrigued by the morpho-ecology of the river patterns, led me to discover Hans-Henrik Stølum's 1996 article entitled "River Meandering as a Self-Organization Process." Stølum's article was among the first to describe the procedural algorithms by which scientists and ecologists today are able to either predict or to reconstruct a particular river's morphology. This morphology, or 'sinuosity,' is the total length and shape of each of a river's arcs, meanders, bends, and reaches.

I set out then to create a site-specific work that could emulate the sinuous shape and flow of a natural river path. The river shape I used was derived from applying the self-organizing meandering river mathematics formula to the topology of an exhibition space. The result was Meandering River - a sculptural installation that wound through the Brandts Art Center in Odense, Denmark in an exhibit entitled Shared Robotics (Fall 2009). The fabrication of Meandering River took place over the three-month duration of the exhibition. A robot was employed to carve river patterns into the surface of a 'stream' of thermal screen material. (The thermal screen material was a flexible, low-density polyethylene-based plastic textile, supplied in rolls 2 feet wide by 250 feet in length.) As the stream of screen material was processed by the robot, it would spill into the exhibition hall where myself and the exhibition staff would arranged it - pushing and pulling the pliable folds until they fit the sinuous lines of the Meandering River. The river eventually traversed the large hall, filling it with the abundant free-flow of arcs along which the river system would 'naturally' follow in that particular space. We used over 2500 feet of thermal screen to complete this first installation of the Meandering River at the Brandts Art Center.

Where the sculptural river met a wall of the exhibition hall, the piece was designed to potentially cascade out a window, thus creating a waterfall of material that would 'run' down the exterior of the building. This configuration was intended not as just a dramatic conclusion to the piece, but as a functional design that would help to cut energy costs by insulating the gallery building's facade and internal climate. The thermal screen material that made up the Meandering River is a product manufactured

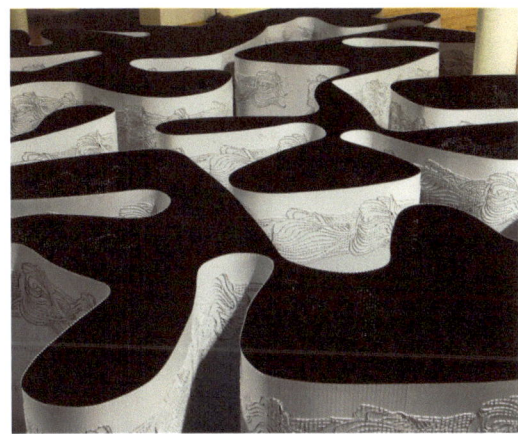

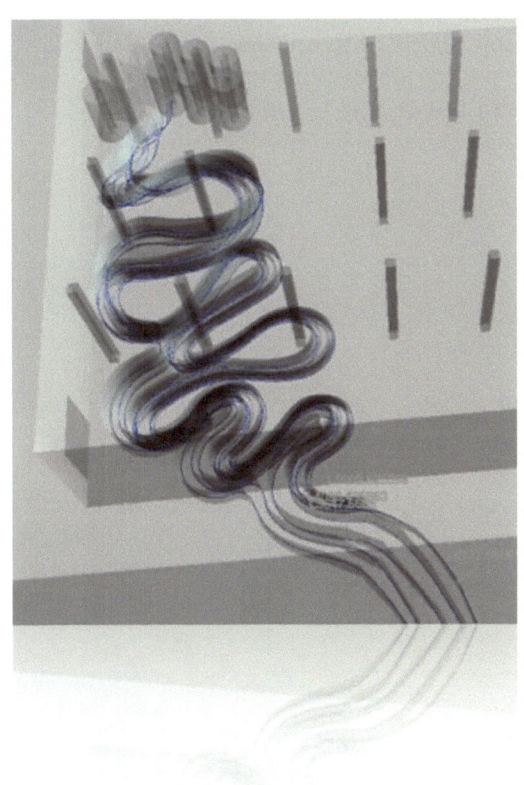

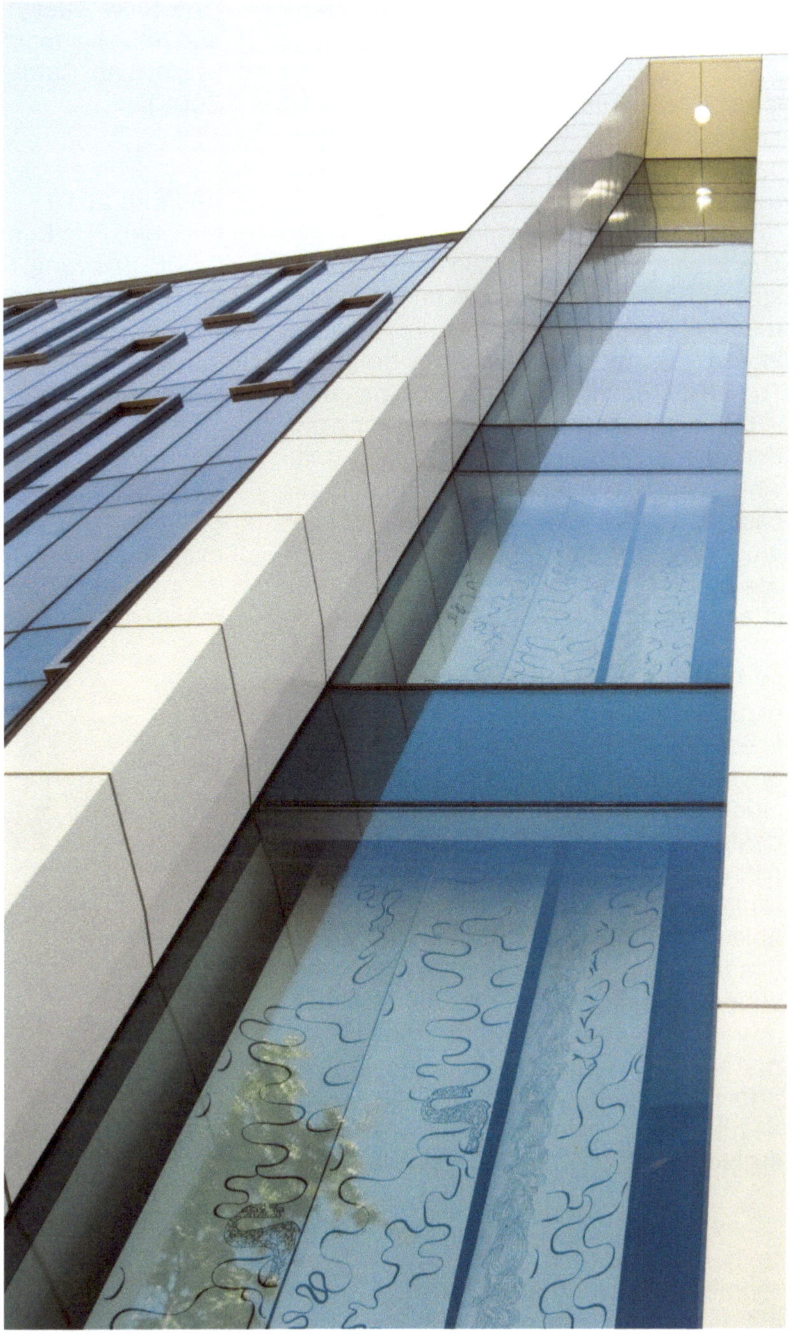

specifically for use as a 'thermal curtain' on the interior or exterior of a building's walls. A hanging thermal curtain typically is used to insulate a space from extreme heat or cold, as well as to help maintain consistent humidity levels within a structure's interior.

The Meandering River cascades down Atkinson Hall's north-facing windows, where the Calit2 gallery is located, fulfilling the intended waterfall outcome for the piece. The next step in the life-cycle of this piece is to make use of this long, cascading portion of the 'river' as a trellis system upon which climbing vines may take root. In this case, a reverse flow of plant material may grow vertically along - and eventually fill - the etched river designs cut by the robot into the thermal screen surface.

In the end, materials and final design of the Meandering River installation fulfilled the sustainable design properties originally laid out for the project which included structural versatility, open source design, and variability of function. The piece is flexible in that it is capable of arrangement as an ever unfolding, drapeable, and expandable artwork. It may be used as both a thermal screen and as a support framework for the cultivation of a vertical garden. The thermal screen material offers also the benefits of being affordable, readily available, lightweight, aesthetically pleasing, environmentally stable, durable, and 100% recyclable.

"Slow design considers the real and potential "expressions" of artifacts and environments beyond their perceived functionalities, physical attributes and lifespans."

(The Slow Design Principles: A new interrogative and reflexive tool for design research and practice by slowLab: Carolyn F. Strauss, Alastair Fuad-Luke, 2008)

(n)-Fold, 2010
Material: FDA Compliant, Food-Grade Polyethylene (LDPE) Sheeting, Dew Condensing Film, Aluminum, Solar Paneling, PVC foam insulation
Dimensions: 22"h x 17"w x 17"d, or variable
Video Animation: duration: 02:05 mins, dimensions: 720 x 480

Pronounced "enfold," (n)-fold is a flat-foldable sculpture and a utilitarian travel system. I began designing the (n)-fold system after my research on river morphology (in conjunction with the Meandering River Project) led me to publications on water scarcity and new water harvesting techniques.

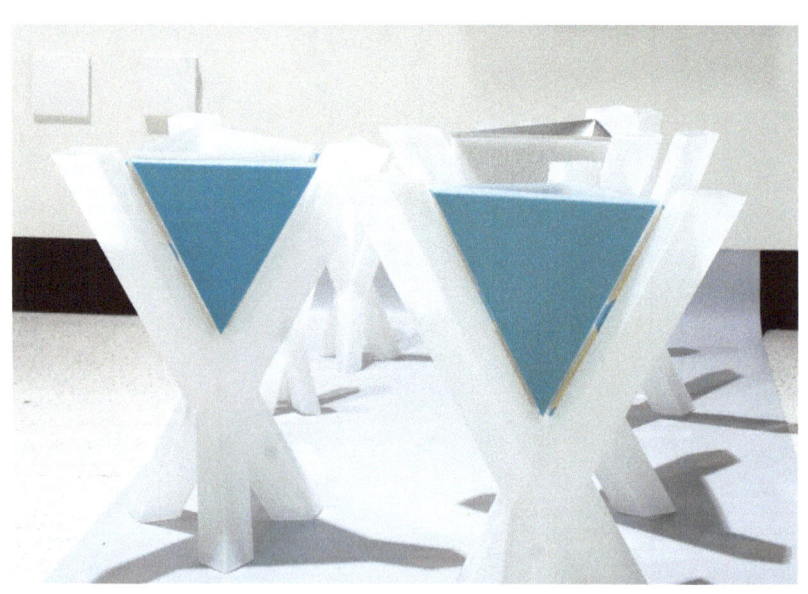

What I found is that, while there is now a plethora of relatively affordable rainwater catchment systems on the market, almost all these relied on the presence of static, Western-style structures to be used as a physical support for the water harvesting system. Specifically, most required either a smooth, pitched roof and/ or a gutter system for rainwater to be routed along, eventually draining into a catchment system (or rain barrel). And, while these systems work well for irrigation or gardening purposes, they are generally not efficient for drinking water collection in that they often render the water non-potable. Rainwater naturally washes debris (dust, dirt, bird feces, etc.) down along roof and along gutter paths as it makes its way to the catchment. Any water collected would necessarily then have to be put through several layers of filtration in order to make it potable again.

The lack of water harvesting techniques by which an individual traveler (or nomad) might collect and purify drinking water as they move through a water scarce region was surprising to me. In fact, I discovered only a handful of techniques currently being employed to collect water that did not rely on static, gutter-based structures. This handful of techniques included fog harvesting, cloud harvesting, and various 'straw' style filters for use with stagnant water. Of those techniques, only one stood out as viable in arid climates and this was dew water harvesting. Today, only a small number of researchers and international organizations are dedicated to making dew water harvesting a more widespread method for water collection – which makes this an especially interesting area to begin work in.

To formulate a vision for (n)-fold, I focused on the concept of portability and on the exploration of the contemporary relationship between individual traveler/ landscape/ and environment. Dew water harvesting, because it can be done on a small scale and in arid climates, lends itself well to design crafted for personal (i.e. individual) use. The challenge was, how to create a sculptural form that could be collapsible, lightweight and durable, and serve as an efficient dew water-harvesting system?

Inspiration came from crease and fold patterns found in traditional origami forms as well as from contemporary flat-packing techniques. Here I found solutions on how to achieve structures that were beautifully versatile on both a physical and a mathematical level. Most fortunately, these structures required only modest materials in order to be fabricated. After testing many different possible fold patterns, eventually the (n)-fold form took shape. It is a pattern that easily folds down into a small, flat profile and which can just as easily unfold, in a flower-like manner, to reveal a large surface area for dew harvesting. The origami-inspired form of (n)-fold has a minimal material weight. Its structure is made of an FDA-compliant, food-grade polyethylene onto which, when unfolded, the dew condensing film hangs.

Further testing and observation on the (n)-fold form revealed its potential to serve as a modular housing element with multiple other uses. When unfolded, the three sides which make up the 'bowl' portion of the structure sit at a 30 degree angle to the sun. This is both an optimal angle for collecting the sun's rays in the form of heat for solar cooking, and in the form of energy for a solar-paneled charging station. The shape of (n)-fold further lends itself to arrangement as an array, which together create an effective automated shade canopy (i.e., thermal screen) for use across building façades.

The flat-packable (n)-fold form and its series of applications are currently in the prototyping stage. Initial prototyping of the first (n)-fold array was completed for the Light Green Light exhibition in collaboration with CRCA (the Center for Research in Computing and the Arts) and the MAE (Mechanical and Aerospace Engineering Program) fabrication lab at UCSD (University of California, San Diego). Currently I am also researching the effectiveness of using passive solar (UV) exposure in the process of purifying the dew water as it is collected.

Light Green Light, 2010 (in collaboration with Travis Saul)
Video Animation: duration: 02:25 mins, dimensions: 720 x 480

Light Green Light (LGL) is the newest artwork to be included in the Light Green Light series and is still in its prototype stage. Similar to (n)-fold, this piece was conceived as an explorative merger between traveler aesthetics, foldable structure design, and functional sculpture. The concept behind LGL is to create a portable lamp, the housing of which may be unfolded to serve as a sleeping habitat for one traveler.

While in Denmark for my residency with Gibotech (2009), it was impossible to avoid a certain measure of immersion into Danish design culture. In that culture

I found that, even today, lamp design remains king. From the flat-foldable Danish lampshade craft of the early 60's to contemporary iterations of famous Poulsen lamp designs, one finds an extraordinary array of collapsible, modular light structures on the Danish market. These structures assemble together like delicate Chinese puzzles and are most often made from sustainable materials.

I felt compelled to try my hand at designing a lamp that could do more than just light, but that could also unpack into a flexible, minimalist living environment. I teamed up with artist Travis Saul to plan out the mechanical engineering of a kinetic structure that would make such a lamp system possible. We tested many different foldaway mechanisms and finally settled on a branching framework that, when collapsed, was capable of folding cloth material down several scales to fit within a multi-tiered lampshade. This cloth, we decided, should be comprised of mosquito netting so that the lamp's integral environment would remain light and translucent - and could also serve as a genuinely utilitarian habitat for a traveler both indoors and outdoors. We also added in a solar interface to the lamp so that the illumination given off by it may be powered by solar energy that is collected during the day.

At this point, we've animated the Light Green Light to show how the unit transforms in shape. The LCL lamp form is one that is versatile and capable of dual applied purposes. It lights a space and provides a traveler with a flexible architecture in which to rest. The materials that will be used in the final production of this piece (such as the mosquito netting) are cost-effective and effective in accentuating both the formal appeal and the functionality of this lamp-based habitat system.

CATALOG N°9
ESSAY BY SABRINA RAAF

OPPOSITE, LIGHT GREEN LIGHT VIDEO INSTALLATION, 2010

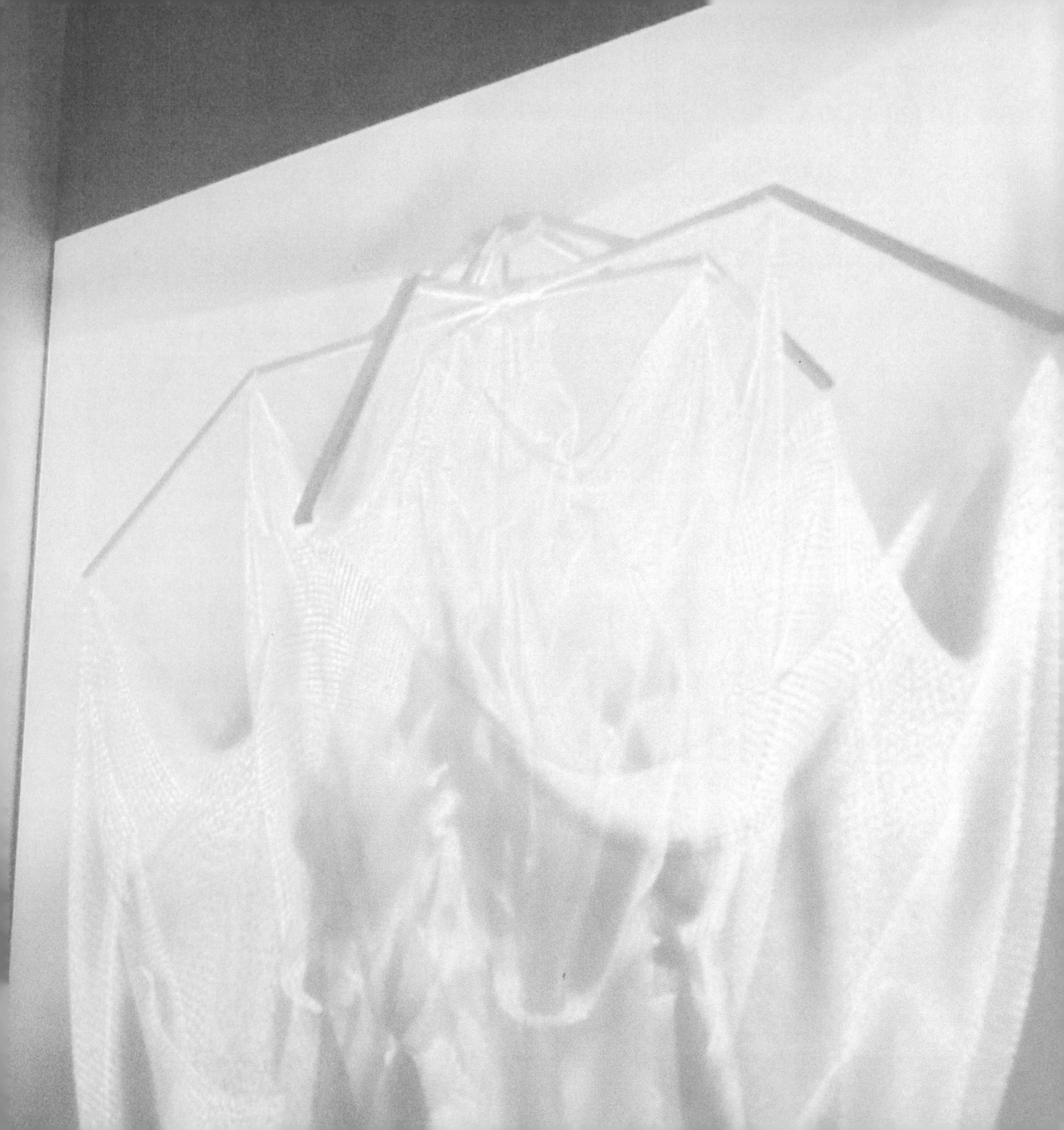

EXHIBITION IMAGES

PLATES

Translator II: Grower, 2004-6

Dimensions: 2'h x 2'w x 17"d
Materials: custom mechanics, aluminum, sensors, and ink
Funding: This project was made possible by a grant from the Creative Capital Foundation, NYC

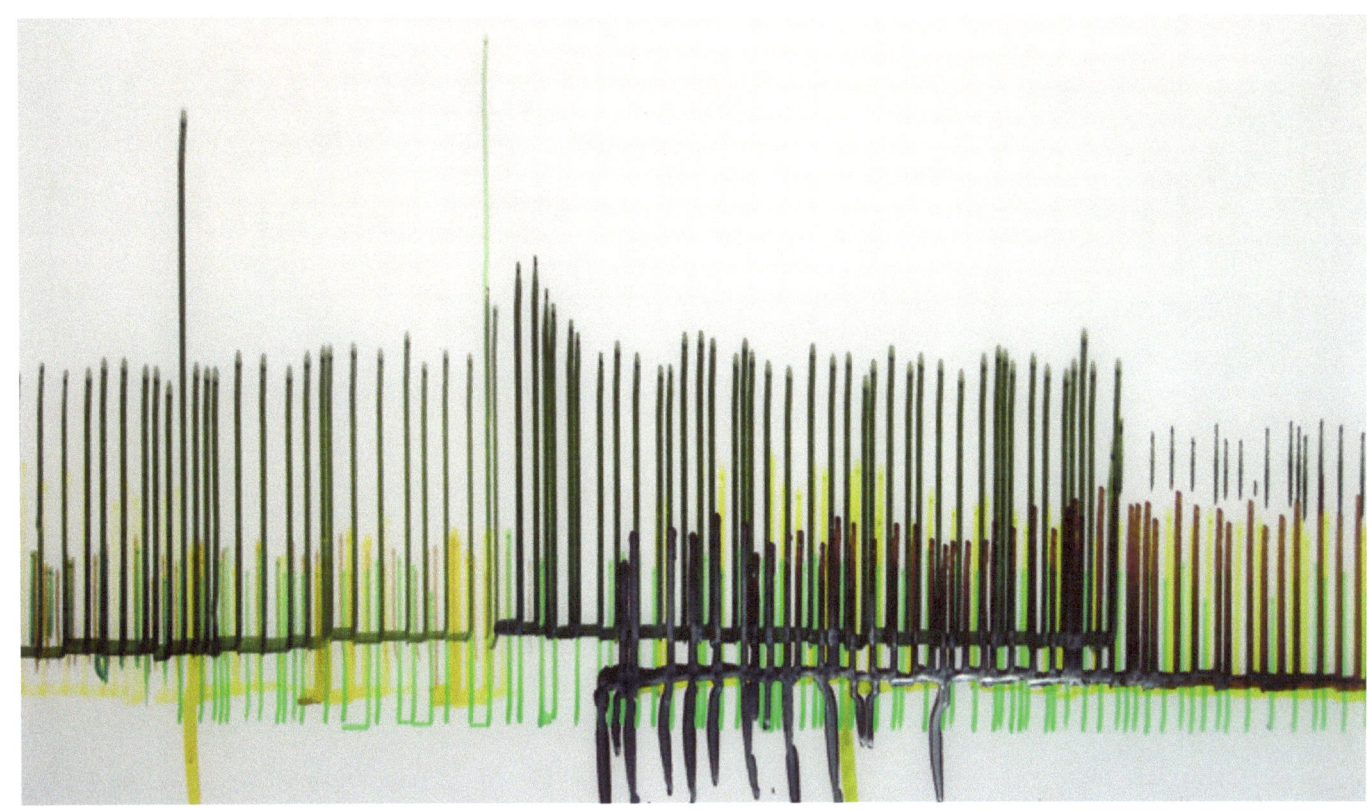

Icelandic RIft, 2006

Dimensions: 45"L x 60"w x 48"h
Materials: aluminum, ferrofluid, plexi, custom electronics

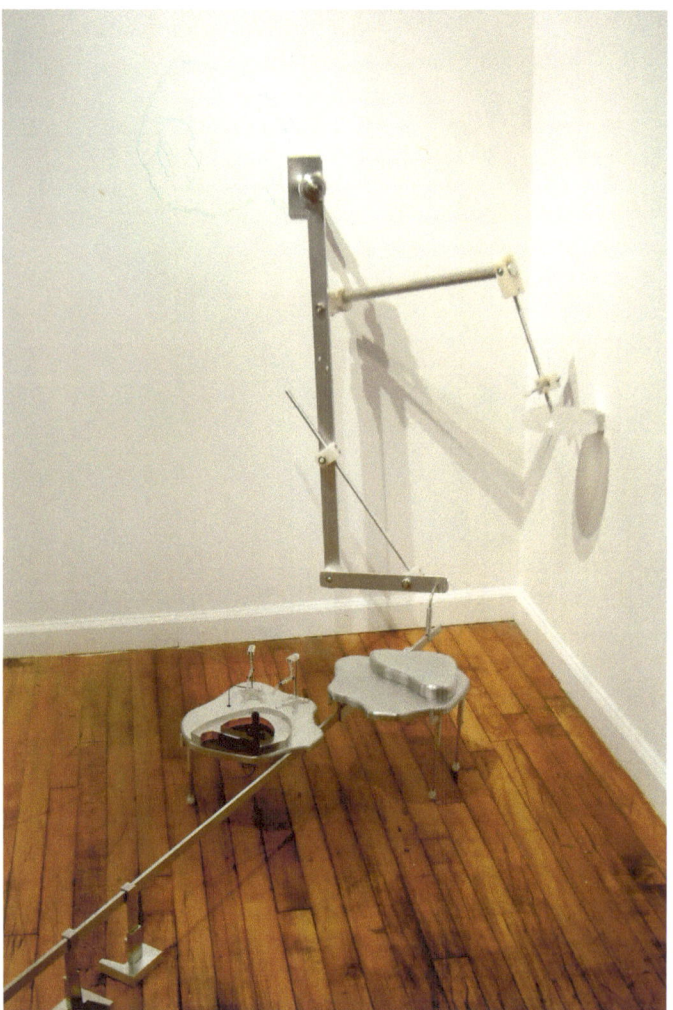

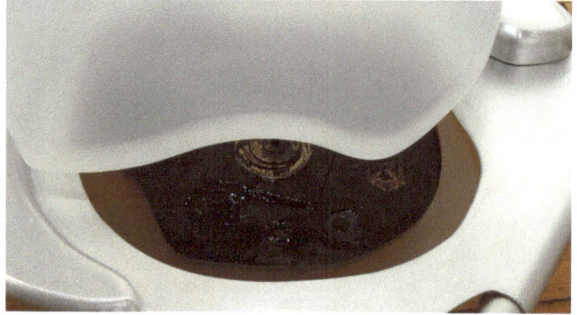

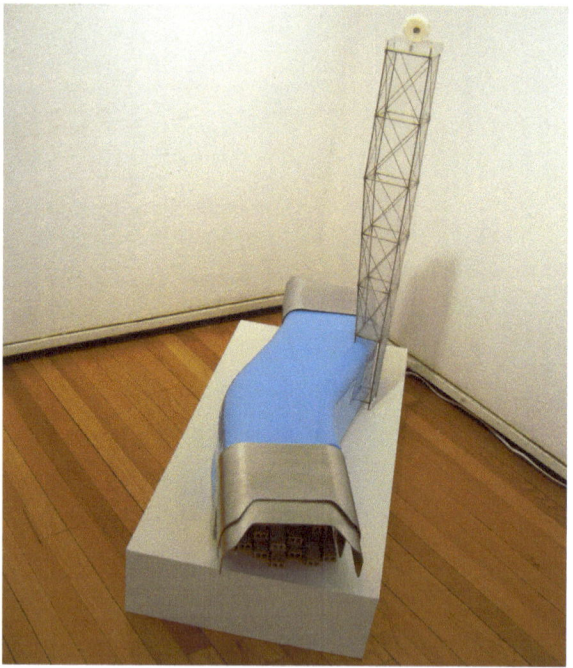

ABOVE, ICELANDIC RIFT, 2006-7 (PHOTOS COURTESY OF SABRINA RAAF)

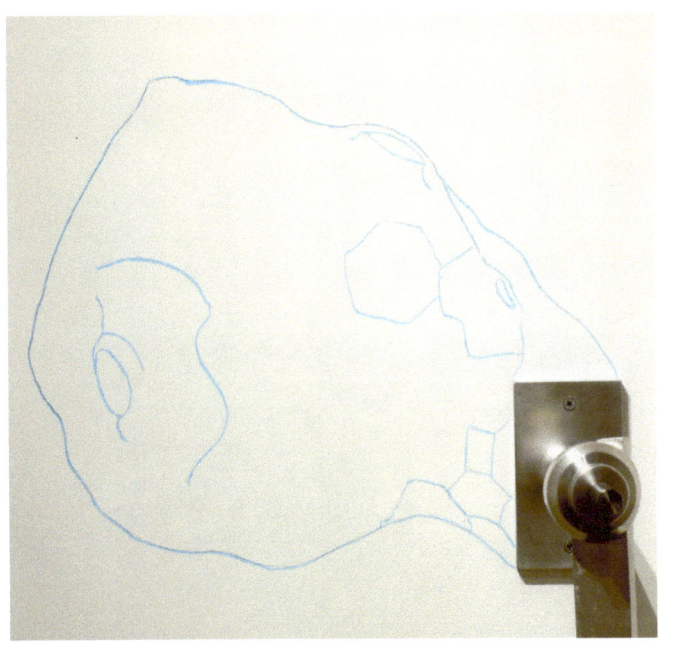

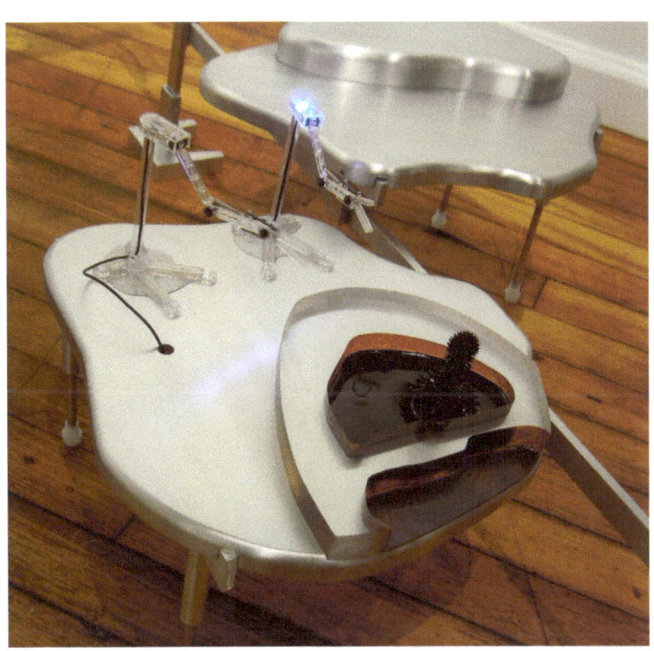

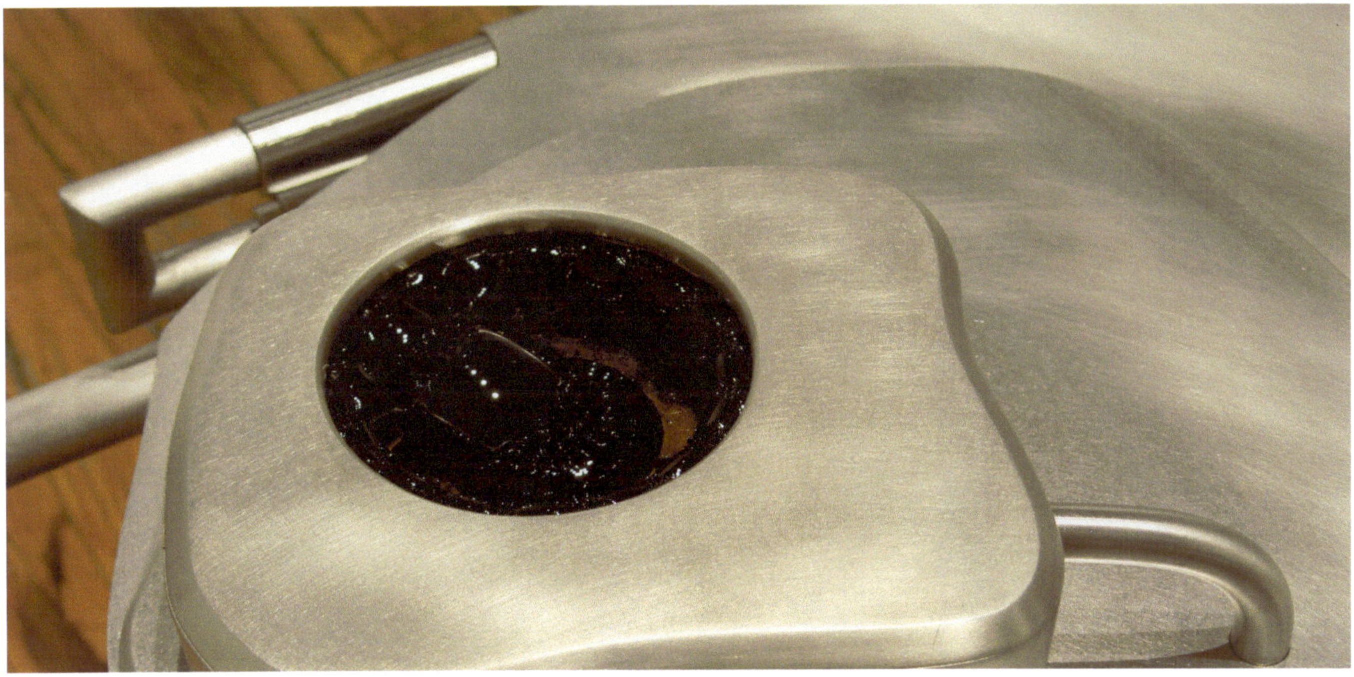

Light Green Light, 2010 (in collaboration with Travis Saul)

Video Animation: duration: 02:25 mins, dimensions: 720 x 480
Installation: In Progress

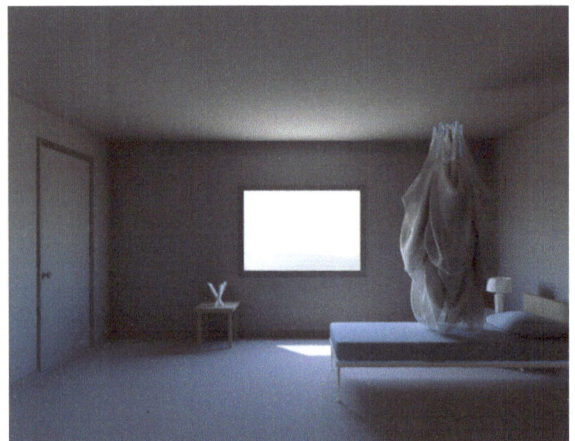
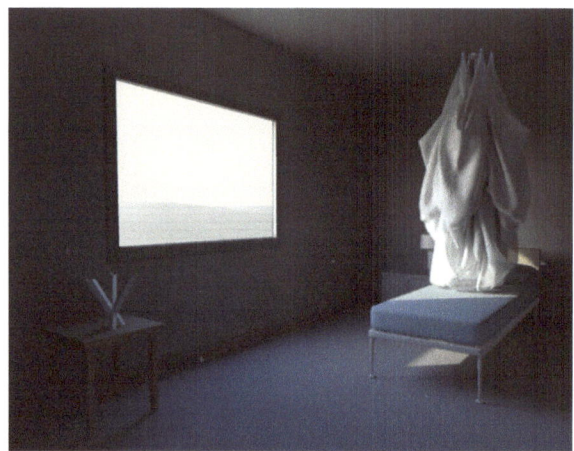
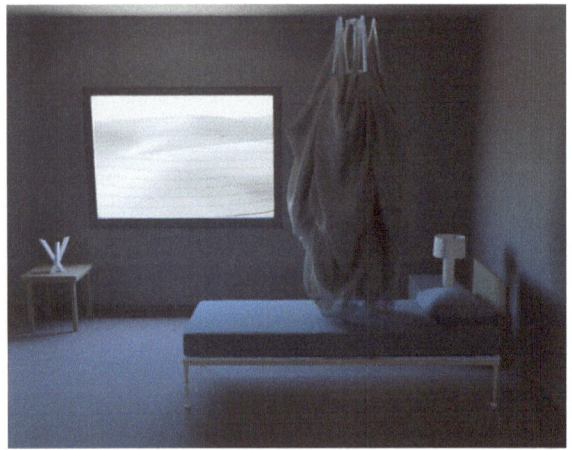
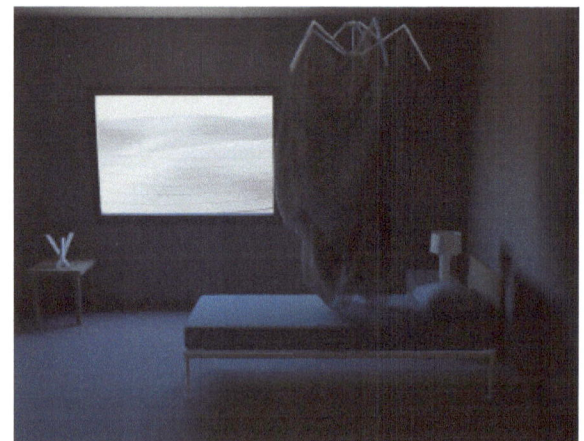

CATALOG N°9
EXHIBITION IMAGES

ABOVE, LIGHT GREEN LIGHT VIDEO STILLS, 2010

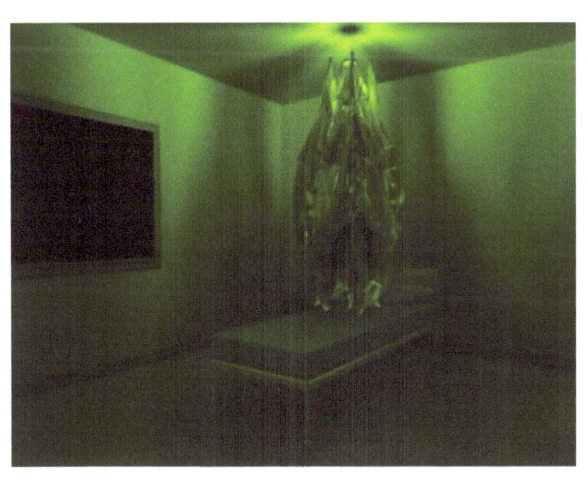
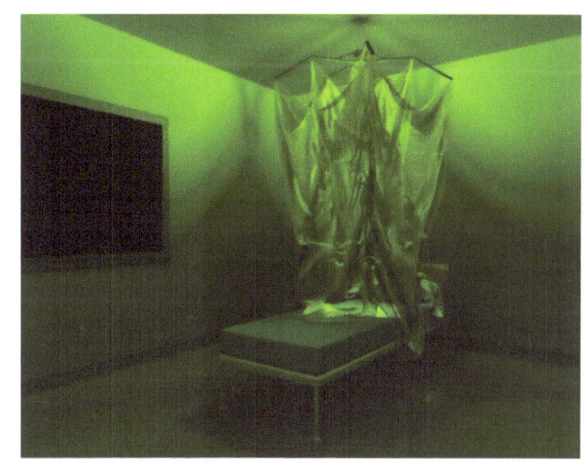
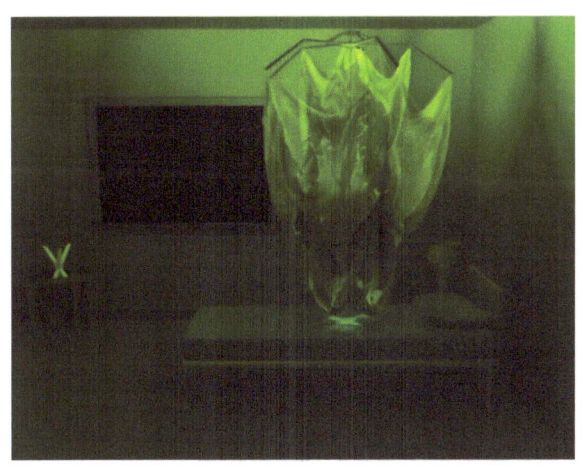
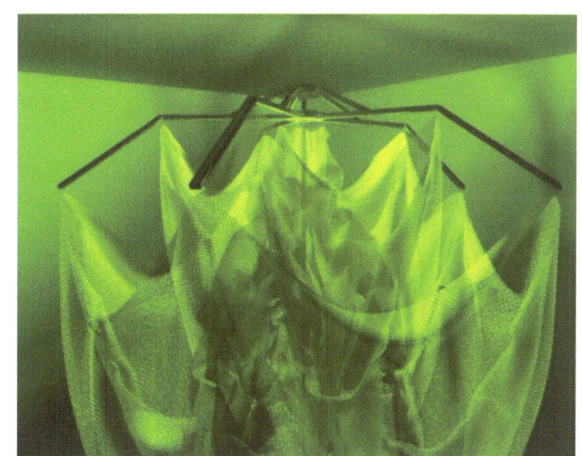

Meandering River, 2009-10

Dimensions: 24" wide x length variable
Materials: Robotically-etched, Thermal Screen (of recyclable HDPE) with vinyl application

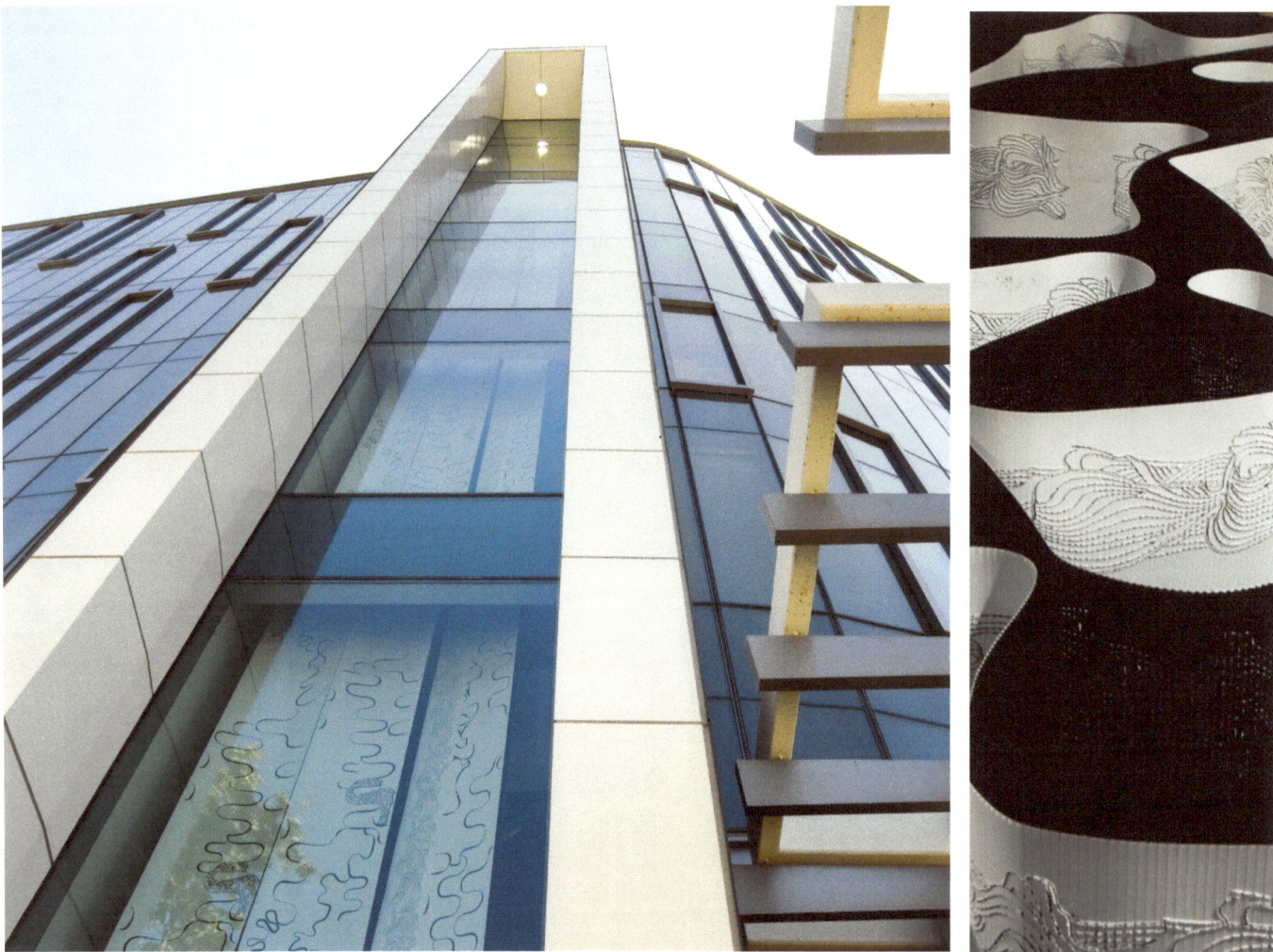

CATALOG N°9
EXHIBITION IMAGES

ABOVE, MEANDERING RIVER, 2010 (PHOTOS COURTESY OF ERIK JESPEN, MAGNUS KASLOV AND SABRINA RAAF)

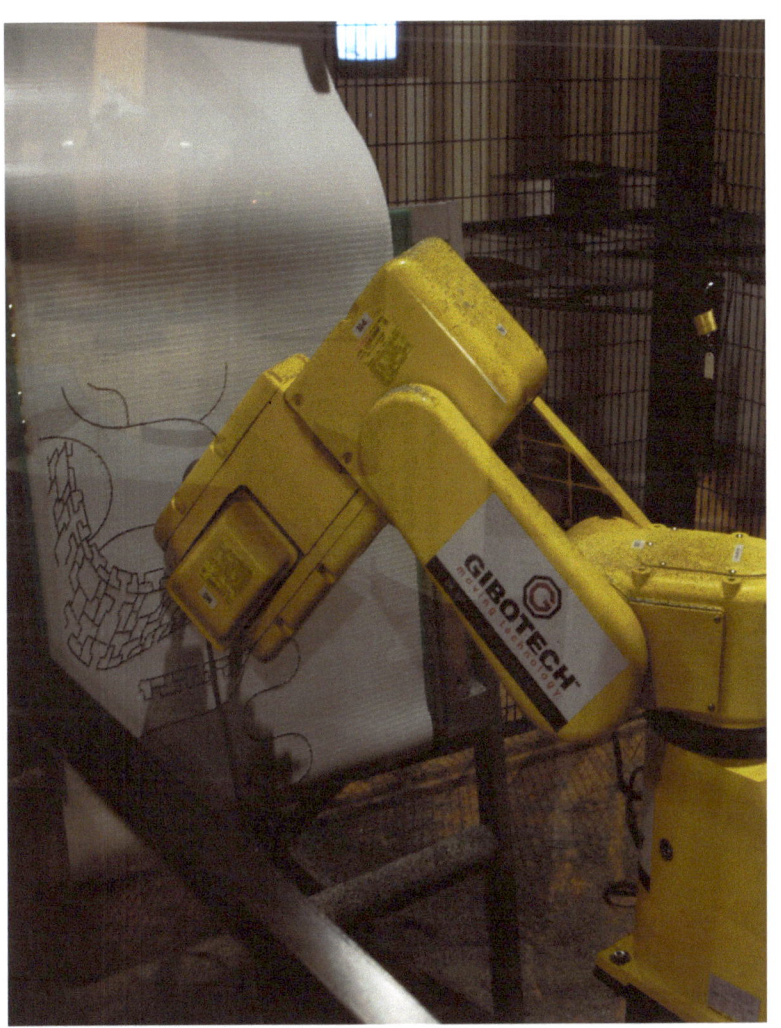

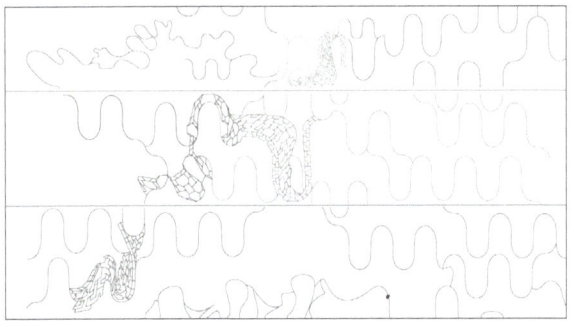

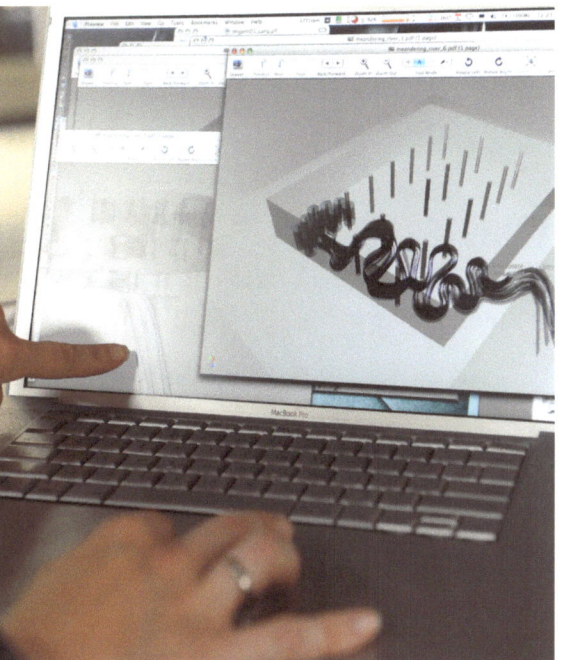

(n)-Fold, 2010

Dimensions: 22"h x 17"w x 17"d, or variable
Material: FDA Compliant, Food-Grade Polyethylene (LDPE) Sheeting, Dew Condensing Film, Aluminum, Solar Paneling, PVC foam insulation
Video Animation: duration: 02:05 mins, dimensions: 720 x 480

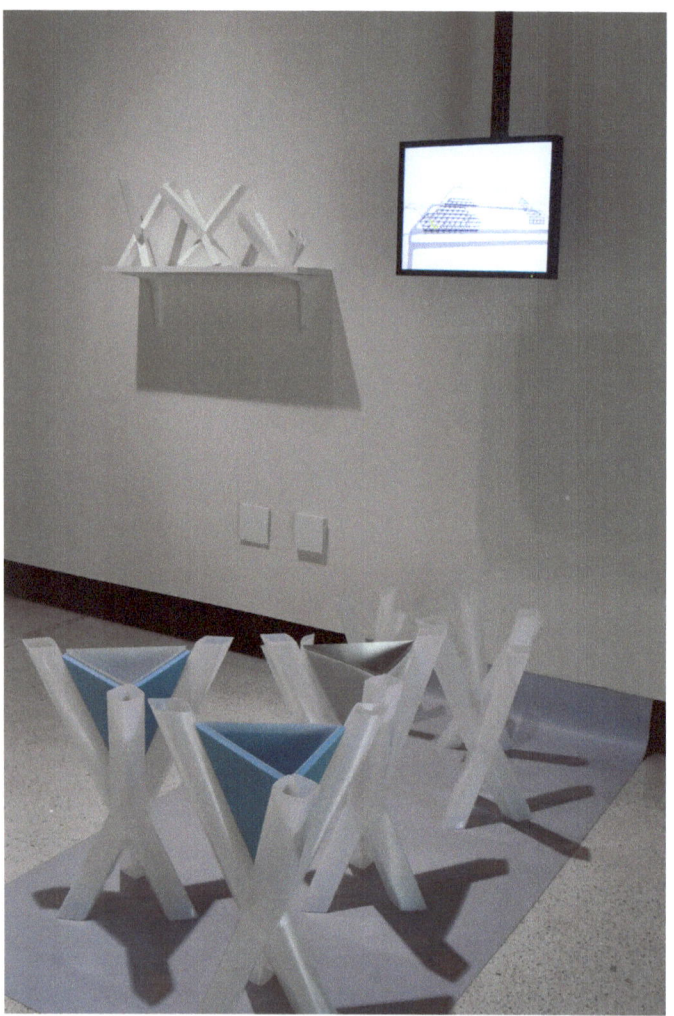
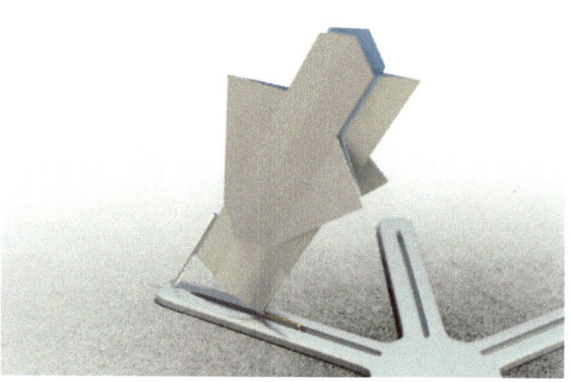
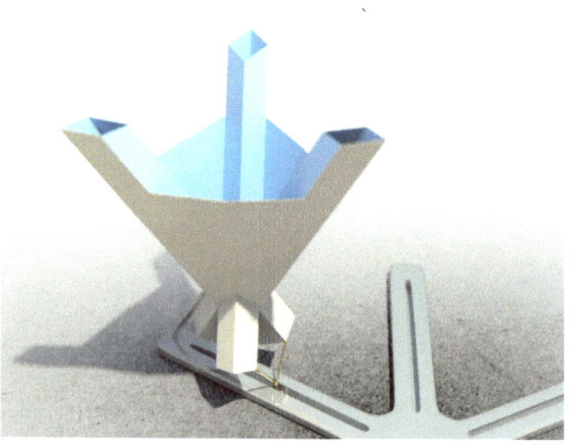

ABOVE, (N)-FOLD INSTALLATION AND VIDEO STILLS, 2010 (PHOTOS COURTESY OF ERIK JESPEN)

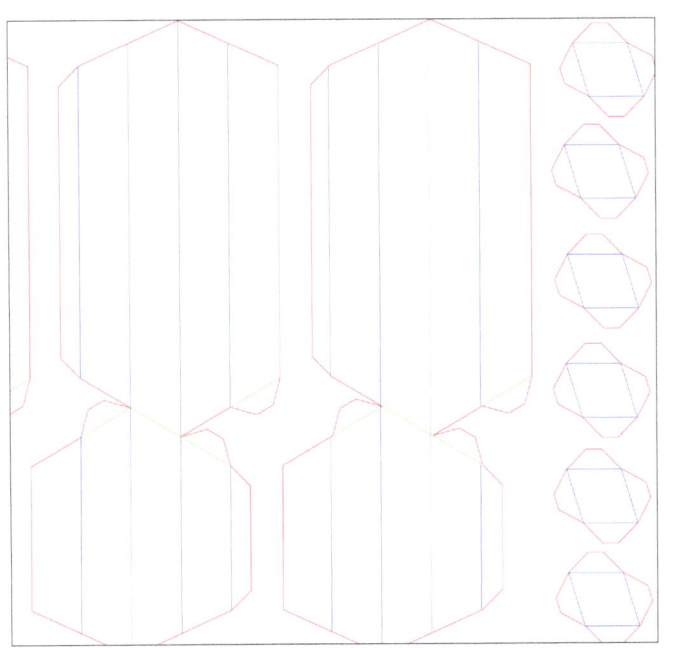

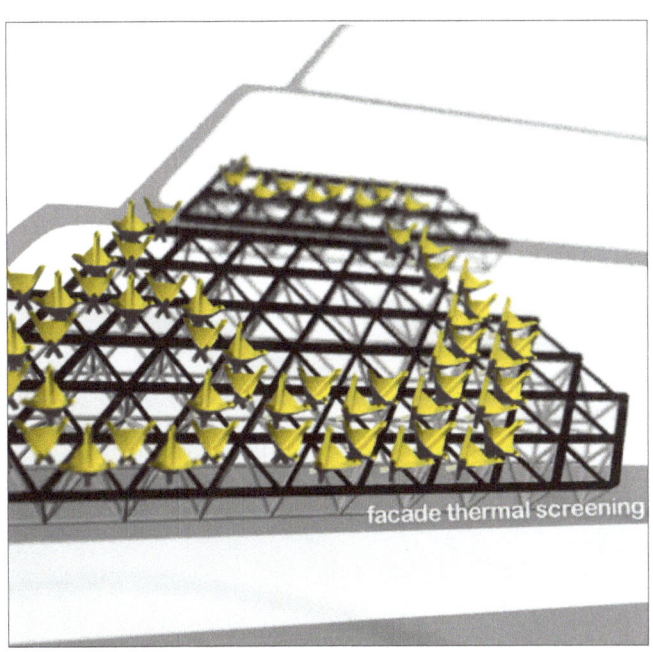

facade thermal screening

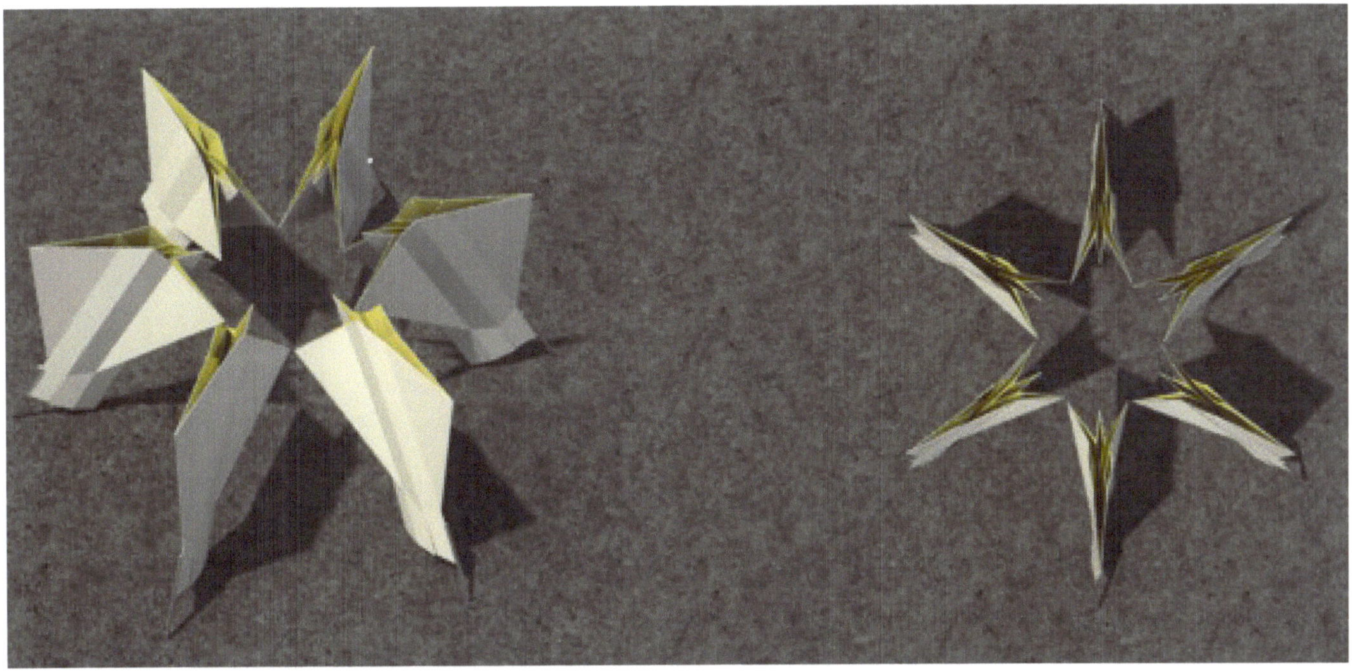

INTERVIEW

BY LARA BULLOCK WITH STEVE DIETZ

Why did you choose these five specific pieces for this show? How do you see the pieces working together?

These five works represent a continuum, from more speculative - the Icelandic Rift series - to work that is directly representational but nevertheless largely symbolic - Translator II: Grower - to Sabrina's latest work, which retains, I would suggest, much of the speculative/symbolic/poetic aspects of this earlier work but also attempts to address in some pragmatic sense issues such as a building's environment through urban (vertical) gardening, water accessibility and solar energy, and malaria through domestic "furniture." Together these works represent a sophisticated design sensibility, which is so critical for creating a cultural context that is conducive to and supportive of change, with a probing engagement with the world.

Why did you choose Sabrina? What was it you saw in Sabrina that made you want to work with her for this project at Calit2?

I knew I wanted to present work where the art was a kind of probe of issues the artist was committed to, but which wasn't only about constructing a better water filter or mosquito netting or whatever the issue was. As is often said, art is as much about asking questions as answering them, while arguably engineering is the opposite. I wanted to present work that engaged engineering (scientific, technological, computational) issues, so to speak, as well as the cultural, aesthetic, social, political worlds that we necessarily live in. When I first met Sabrina in person

- I had known some of her work for some time - I listened to this incredibly detailed and knowledgeable discourse about engineering, mathematics, computer programming, robotics, and ecology - while looking at these really beautiful and poetic projects that rigorously utilized these disciplines, among others, to present a compelling vision of a possible future.

The title of the exhibition, A Light Green Light: Towar Sustainability in Pactice, is extremely provocative. The first part of the subtitle, Toward Sustainability, suggests a movement toward something. What did you mean by this phrase? How did you intend for this movement to come across . . . and why did you specify "Sustainability in Practice" versus, say, in "life"?

I think we're still trying to understand what sustainability means and so there is a kind of trajectory toward something that probably hasn't been fully achieved at this point. At the same time, we often speak of an artist's "practice," and one way to think about Sabrina's work is as a practice that is not only about sustainability, but also, at least with regard to this particular selection, how to sustain a certain artistic vision in the face of monumental challenges to humanity. Finally, practice is meant in relation to failure. "Practice makes perfect." Perhaps not, but in the sciences "failure" can be as informative or more so than "success," and I think that part of trying to figure out sustainability, part of trying to figure out one's practice is to learn from experience, and I think that's powerfully present in Sabrina's work as well. Learning, not just repeating what is known - and known to be successful.

Often with media arts, there is a questionable line between art and design. How do you both see art and technology engaging with other methodological discourses? Is it important that the work extend beyond the gallery?

I sometimes call this an "edge condition." An edge is a boundary - divide between this or that - but an edge condition is an intersection, not only of, for example, art and design or art and technology, but of physical and virtual, conceptual and actual, future and present, familiar and experimental, real and imagined. It can be discomfiting and disorienting. An edge condition is like an estuary where the river meets the ocean - not quite either but teeming with evolved adaptations.

As a curator, I am agnostic about whether it is important a specific work extends beyond the gallery. That is an artistic choice not a condition of art.

How do you view the link between art and technology?

As an edge condition.

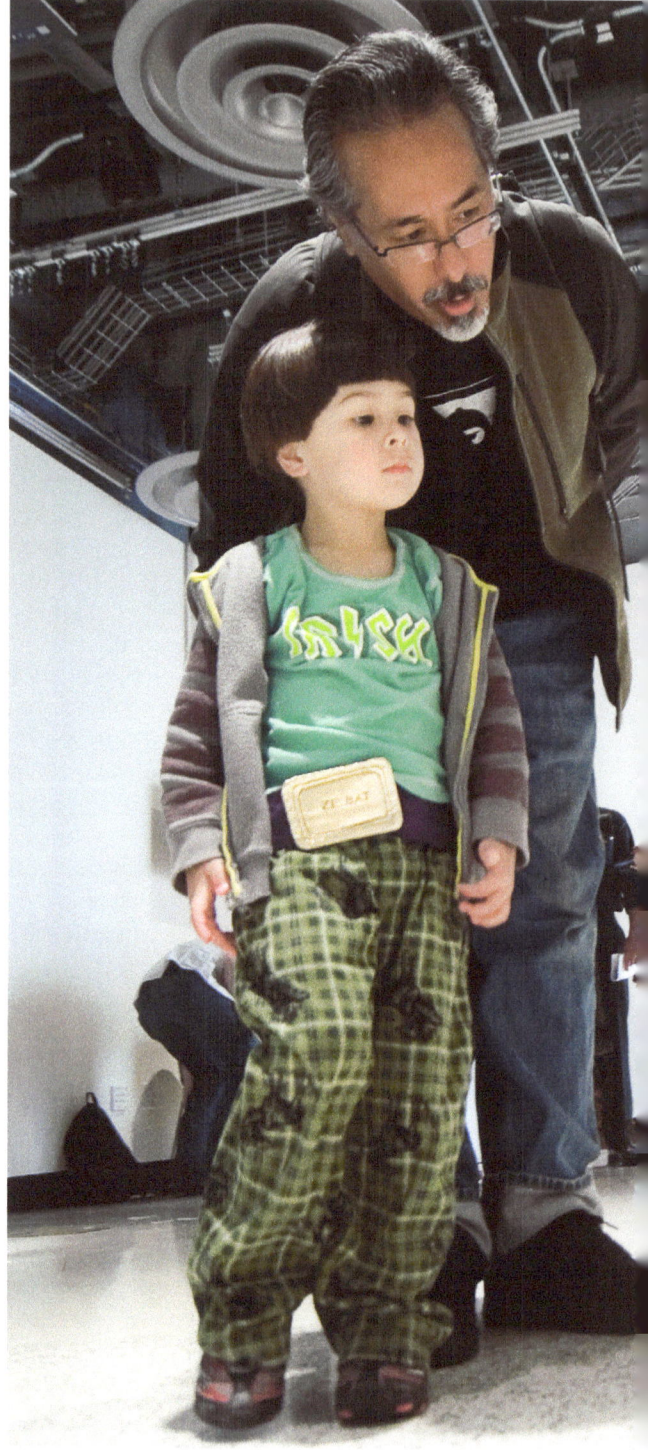

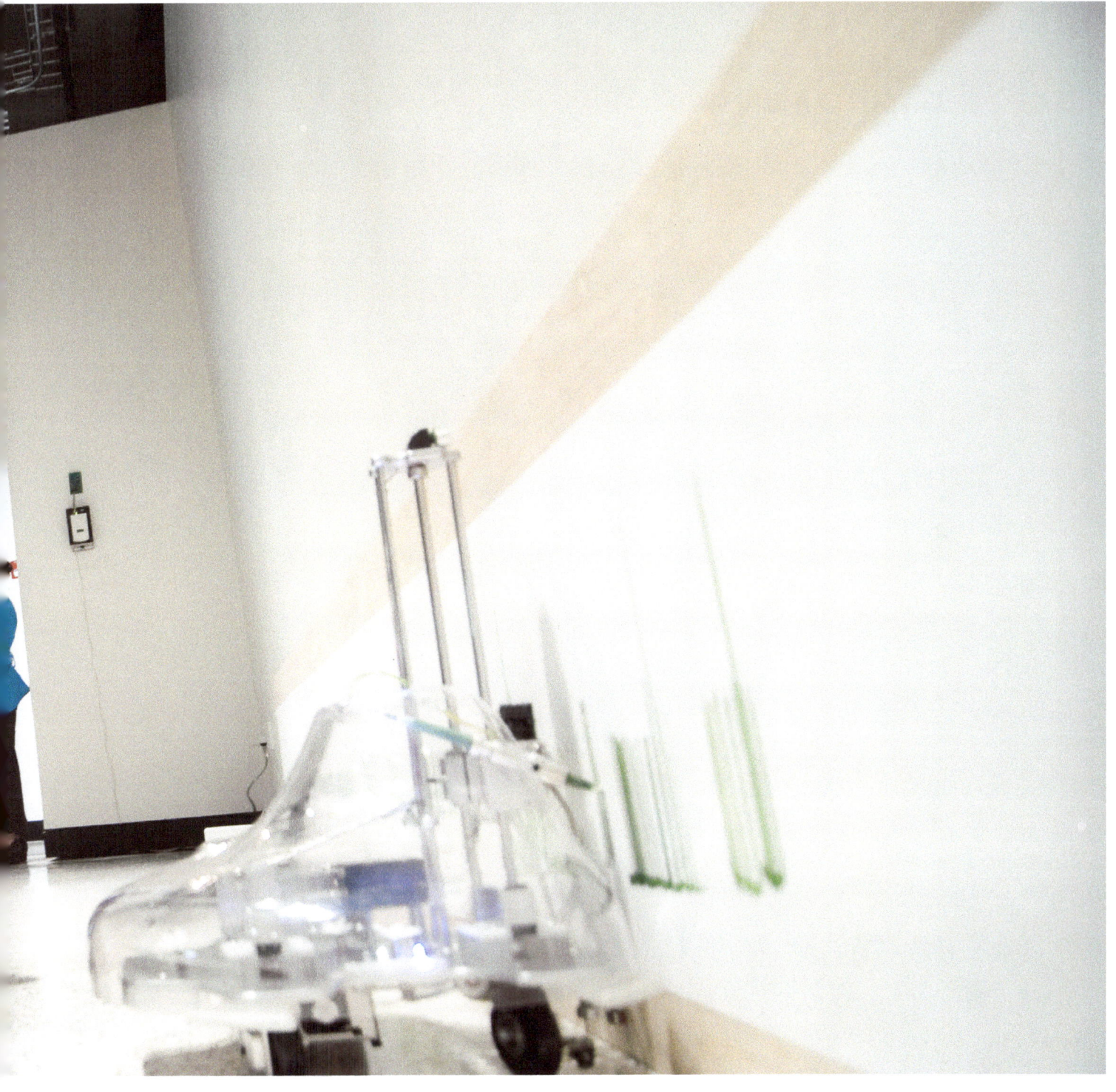

ARTIST BIOGRAPHY

SABRINA RAAF

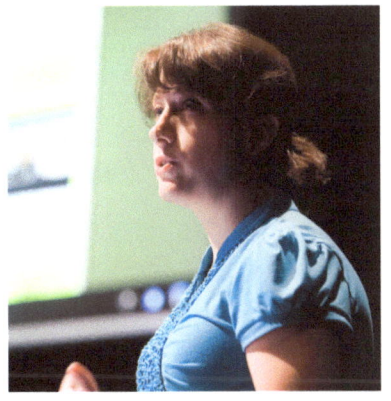

Sabrina Raaf, a Chicago-based artist, works in experimental sculptural media and also designs responsive environments and social spaces. Her work has been presented in solo and group exhibitions at the Brandts Art Center (Denmark), Transitio_MX (Mexico City), Sala Parpalló (Spain), MejanLabs (Stockholm), Lawimore Projects (Seattle), the Edith-Russ-Site for Media Art (Germany), Stefan Stux Gallery (NYC), Ars Electronica (Linz), Museum Tinguely (Basel), Espace Landowski (Paris), Kunsthaus Graz (Austria), and ISEA 2004 (Helsinki). She was the recipient of a Creative Capital Grant in Emerging Fields (2002) and an Illinois Arts Council Fellowship (2005 &2001). Reviews of her work have appeared in Art in America, Contemporary, Chicago Tribune Sunday Magazine, Leonardo, The Washington Post, and New Art Examiner. She received an MFA in Art and Technology from the School of the Art Institute of Chicago (1999) and is currently an Associate Professor in the School of Art and Design at the University of Illinois at Chicago.

CURATOR BIOGRAPHY

STEVE DIETZ

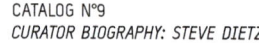

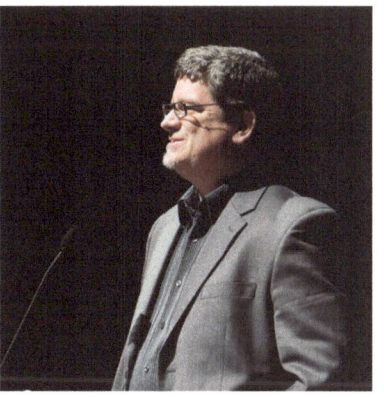

Steve Dietz is Founder, President, and Artistic Director of Northern Lights.mn. He was the Founding Director of the biennial 01SJ Global Festival of Art on the Edge in 2006 and is currently Artistic Director of its producing organization, ZERO1: the Art and Technology Network. He is the former Curator of New Media at the Walker Art Center in Minneapolis, Minnesota, where he founded the New Media Initiatives department in 1996, the online art Gallery 9 and digital art study collection. He also co-founded, with the Minneapolis Institute of Arts the award-winning educational site ArtsConnectEd, and the artist community site mnartists.org with the McKnight Foundation. Dietz founded one of the earliest, museum-based, independent new media programs at the Smithsonian American Art Museum in 1992.

ACKNOWLEDGMENTS

"A Light Green Light: Toward Sustainability in Practice", featuring the artwork of Sabrina Raaf and curated by Steve Dietz, has been one of the most ambitious exhibitions that we've held at the gallery@calit2. The exhibition would not have been possible without the support of the community at Calit2, the insight of the gallery committee, and the involvement of collaborators across campus. In addition to thanking Steve Dietz, Sabrina Raaf, and Travis Saul for their vision and effort, I would like to acknowledge all those who helped make this exhibition a success. Calit2 UCSD Division Director Ramesh Rao provided valuable resources along with thoughtful guidance to the gallery for this exhibition. Gallery Co-Chairs Ricardo Dominguez and Lea Rudee steered the direction the exhibition would take, guided by a willingness to push the boundaries of what art looks like and can achieve at Calit2.

Invaluable technical support for the installation of "A Light Green Light: Toward Sustainability in Practice" came from Hector Bracho, Mike Toillion, Emily Jankowski, Laura Park, and Sam Doshier. Art installation assistance was provided by Daniel Johnson, Janny Li, and Virginie Dang. Special thanks to Greg Dawe, who helped creatively hang "Meandering River" and Todd Margolis, who aided in the fabrication of the prototypes for "A Light Green Light." Throughout the exhibition, gallery assistants Christina Telya, Joey Ma, Tracy Lederberger, Kent Ngo, Vanessa Neag and Jennifer Delizo carefully maintained the robots in the gallery.

Many thanks are due to Doug Ramsey for editing this publication, Cristian Horta for layout and design, Erik Jepsen for photography, and Alex Matthews for video production. Special thanks to Lara Bullock, for her interview with Steve Dietz, which is included in this catalog.

I would like to extend my gratitude to Yuki Marsden and Tim Beach for permitting the gallery to take advantage of the unique facilities at Atkinson Hall for this exhibition. My deepest appreciation goes out to all the support staff at Calit2, in particular to Lovella Cacho, Mark Plummer, and Dee Chieng for their administrative assistance on behalf of the gallery. Your ongoing efforts enable us to continue to reach out to the students at UCSD as well as the wider arts community, and provide them with a unique, enriching and educational arts experience.

Further thanks go to Andy Graham and Mary Parks at the University of Illinois at Chicago's Innovation Center for their collaboration and guidance on the vinyl pattern fabrication for the Meandering River piece.

- Trish Stone, Gallery Coordinator

Creative Capital

We'd like to extend our gratitude to the Creative Capital Foundation for their generous gift of funding towards the production of this catalog and towards the creation of the artwork, Translator II: Grower. The Creative Capital provides integrated financial and advisory support to artists pursuing adventurous projects in five disciplines: Emerging Fields, Film/Video, Innovative Literature, and Performing and Visual Arts. Working in long-term partnership with artists, Creative Capital's pioneering approach to support combines funding, counsel and career development services to enable a project's success and foster sustainable practices for its grantees. For further information: http://creative-capital.org/

gallery@calit2 reflects the nexus of innovation implicit in Calit2's vision, and aims to advance our understanding and appreciation of the dynamic interplay among art, science and technology.

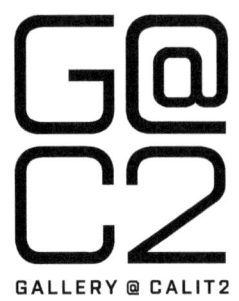

GALLERY @ CALIT2

First Floor
Atkinson Hall
9500 Gilman Drive
University of California, San Diego
La Jolla, CA 92093

http://gallery.calit2.net